THE GOSPEL
OF THOMAS

TRANSLATED BY
JEAN-YVES LELOUP

CALLIGRAPHY BY
FRANK LALOU

SHAMBHALA
Boston & London
2003

SHAMBHALA PUBLICATIONS, INC.
Horticultural Hall
300 Massachusetts Avenue
Boston, Massachusetts 02115
www.shambhala.com

© 2002 Albin Michel
Translation © 2003 Shambhala Publications, Inc.

English translation by Sherab Chödzin Kohn
Collection directed by Jean Mouttapa and Valérie Menanteau
Photography by Sylvie Durand
Layout Design by Céline Julien

9 8 7 6 5 4 3 2 1

First Shambhala Edition
Printed in France by Pollina. L 88312 b

⊛ This edition is printed on acid-free paper that meets the American
National Standards Institute z39.48 Standard.

Distributed in the United States by Random House, Inc.,
and in Canada by Random House of Canada Ltd

LIBRARY OF CONGRESS CATALOGING-IN-PUBLICATION DATA

Gospel of Thomas (Coptic Gospel). English.
The Gospel of Thomas/edited by Jean-Yves Leloup; calligraphy by
Frank Lalou.—1st ed.
p. cm. — (Shambhala calligraphy)
ISBN 1-59030-042-4 (pbk.: alk. paper)
I. Leloup, Jean-Yves. II. Lalou, Frank. III. Title. IV. Series

BS2860.T5 A313 2003
299'.8—dc21   2002011830

T HE GOSPEL OF THOMAS, discovered in 1945 in the region of Nag Hammadi in Upper Egypt, is a collection of one hundred and fourteen *logia* or "naked sayings," attributed to the Master, the Mild, the Living One. These sayings are supposed to have been collected by Didymos Judas Thomas—his twin? His alter ego? (*didymos* means "twin" in Greek). These are not wordy sayings but rather enigmas in the manner of Zen koans, short maxims that are apparently lacking in sense, but which—if one allows them to penetrate like grains of sand into the gears of our ordinary mentality—might provoke a stoppage, a silence, a transformation of consciousness.

This gospel has had a varied reception at the hands of critics. For some it is one more text from among the Apocrypha that is interesting in relation to the study of

Gnosticism. For others it is a hodgepodge of sayings of Jesus, drawn in some cases from the canonical Gospels and in others from heterodox traditions that attribute the sayings to Jesus. And finally for another group of commentators, this gospel is the very source the Gospel writers drew their material from, the "proto-Gospel" of which everyone has dreamed that would transmit to us the only truly authentic sayings of Jesus.

But whether we like it or not, Jesus did not write anything. Therefore there will never be truly authentic sayings of Jesus. Every saying transmitted to us is a "heard saying," that is to say, it retains the imprint of the person who heard it, whether that imprint is crude or subtle. Mark, Matthew, Luke, John, Thomas—and there are many others—provide so many ways of hearing the One Word, of understanding it, of translating it into language, into culture, in accordance with the given writer's intimacy with He who spoke, in accordance with that writer's openness and the development of his field of consciousness. Not one of the ways of hearing can pretend to "contain the Word," because "it is the truth, but not all of it."

The ear of Thomas is certainly less sensitive to Hebraicisms that than that of Matthew, less attentive to the tales of miracles than that of Mark, less careful to register the mercy of God proclaimed "even to the heathens" than Luke. The ear of Thomas is more focused on the teaching that Jesus transmits, each bit of intelligence received from Him being regarded as the seed of the new man, as the genesis of knowledge. It is in this fashion that Thomas or the authors who place themselves under the protection of this "infinitely skeptical and infinitely faithful" apostle make Jesus one of their number, that is to say, a Gnostic.

Jesus, in the manner of masters of the East, invites us by means of paradoxical formulations to become aware of our uncreated origin, of our freedom without limits in the very midst of the most restrictive contingencies. Here it is a question of awakening to the absolute Reality in the very core of relative or deceptive realities. It is an unceasing journey from a limited consciousness to an unlimited consciousness. "Be passers-by," the Gospel of Thomas tells us. A relative knowledge exists, the one we acquire from books, encounters, from the thought of others. There also exists a knowledge "from the very self," from "the living nature that is within you." It is to this knowledge, to this *gnosis*, that Jesus seems to invite us so that we may become like him, not "good Christians," but additional Christs, or additional Gnostics or enlightened ones.

The twenty-four logia in this volume of Shambhala Calligraphy are drawn from the work, *L'Évangile de Thomas*, published by Éditions Albin Michel. For this translation I referred to the Coptic text established by Y. Haas, the Greek retroversion of R. Kasser, as well as the Oxyrhynchus papyrus.

Jean-Yves Leloup

These are the words of the Secret.
Jesus, the Living, revealed them.
Didymos Judas Thomas wrote them down.

LOGION 1

He said:
He who finds
the significance of these words
will not taste death.

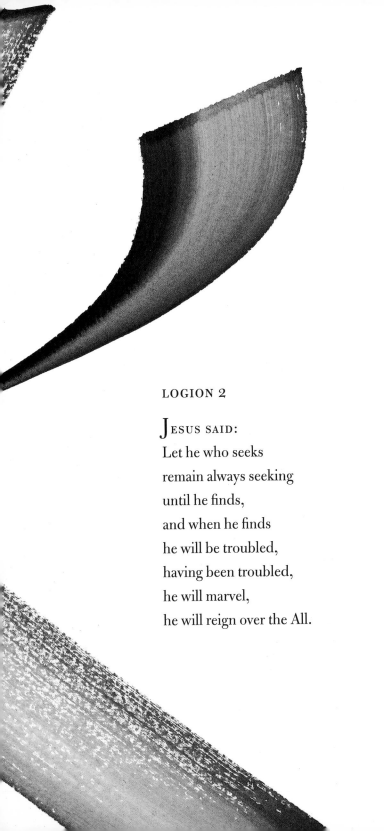

LOGION 2

Jesus said:
Let he who seeks
remain always seeking
until he finds,
and when he finds
he will be troubled,
having been troubled,
he will marvel,
he will reign over the All.

LOGION 3

Jesus said:
If those who guide you assert:
behold, the Kingdom is in the Heavens,
then the birds are closer to it than you;
if they say:
behold, it is in the sea,
then the fishes know it already . . .
The Kingdom: it is within you
and it is outside of you.
When you know yourself,
then you will be known and you will know
that you are the children of the Father, the Living One;
but if you do not know yourself,
you are in the vain
and you are vanity.

ⲀⲈⲞⲨⲚⲀⲒⲦⲚⲀⲘⲰⲢⲦⲚⲀⲢⲒⲀⲈ
ⲀⲨⲰⲚⲤⲈⲰⲰⲠⲈⲞⲨⲞⲨⲰⲦ

LOGION 4

Jⲉsus said:
The old man will not hesitate
to question the child
of seven days as to
the Place of Life, and he will live.
Many of the first
will become last
and they will be One.

LOGION 5

J ESUS SAID:
Recognize that which is
before your face
and that which is hidden from you
will be revealed to you.
There is nothing hidden
that will not be manifest.

ПЄХЄ ІС

ϹΟΥШΝΠЄ ΤΠΗΠΤΟΠΠЄΚΓΟЄ

ΒΟΛΛΥШΠЄΘΗΠЄΡΟΚΥΝΑϬШΛ

ΠЄΒΟΛΝΑΚ·ΤΠΛΛΥΓΑΡЄΥϹΗΤ

ЄΥΝΛΟΥШΝΚЄΒΟΛΛΝ

COOΥ

LOGION 6

HIS DISCIPLES questioned him in this manner:
Must we fast? How should we pray?
How should we give alms?
What must be observed with regard
to food?
Jesus said:
Stop the lie,
that which you do not like, do not do it;
you are naked before Heaven,
that which you hide, that which is veiled,
all will be uncovered.

LOGION 17

Jᴇsᴜs sᴀɪᴅ:
I will give you
what the eye has not seen,
what the ear has not heard,
what the hand has not touched,
what has not arisen
in the heart of man.

LOGION 18

THE DISCIPLES asked Jesus:
Tell us what our end will be.
Jesus replied:
What do you know of the beginning
that you seek the end in this manner?
There where the beginning is,
there will also be the end.

Happy is he who stays
within the beginning;
he will know the end
and he will not taste death.

ΥΜΑΚΑΡΙΟCΠΕΤΝ

THE DISCIPLES asked Jesus:
Tell us what
the Kingdom of Heaven is like:
He said to them:
It is like a mustard seed,
the smallest of all seeds;
when it falls on cultivated ground,
it becomes a great tree
where the birds of Heaven take shelter.

LOGION 25

JESUS SAID:
Love your brother
like your soul,
watch over him
as over the apple
of your eye!

TOTEKNANAYEBON

LOGION 26

JESUS SAID:
The straw
that is in the eye of your brother,
you see it.
But the beam of wood
that is in your eye,
you do not see.
When you remove
the beam from your eye,
then you will see clearly
to remove the straw
that is in the eye
of your brother.

LOGION 33

Jesus said:
That which you hear with one ear,
tell it to another ear,
proclaim it from the rooftops.
No one lights a lamp
to put it under a bushel
or in a hidden place,
but one places it on a lampstand,
so that, from the inside and from the outside,
its light is seen.

LOGION 42
JESUS SAID:
Be passers-by.

LOGION 45

J ESUS SAID:
One does not harvest
grapes from thorn bushes.
One does not pick figs
from thistles,
they do not bear fruit.
The good man,
from the secret of his heart,
produces goodness.
The wicked man,
from the secret of his heart,
produces wickedness.
That which is expressed,
is that which overflows from the heart.

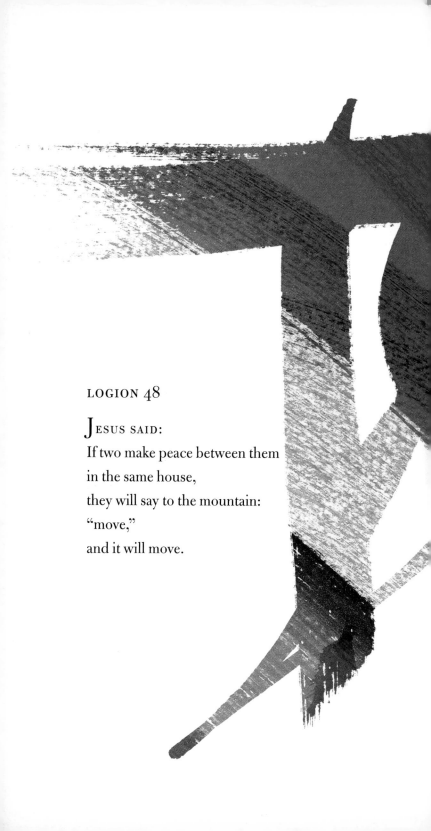

LOGION 48

Jᴇsᴜs sᴀɪᴅ:
If two make peace between them
in the same house,
they will say to the mountain:
"move,"
and it will move.

LOGION 59

J ESUS SAID:
Look toward the One who Lives
while you are living.
Once you are dead, you will seek to see Him
without achieving this vision.

LOGION 61

Jᴇꜱᴜꜱ ꜱᴀɪᴅ:
Two will be lying in one bed,
one will die, the other will live.
Salomé questioned him:
Who are you, man,
where do you come from? From whom
    were you born
that you climb upon my bed
and eat at my table?
Jesus said to her:
I am he who has come forth
from He who is Openness.
I was given what came from my Father.
Salomé replied: I am your disciple.
Jesus said to her:
That is why I say
when the disciple is open,
he is filled with light.
When he is divided,
he is filled with darkness.

LOGION 72

A MAN SAID to Jesus:
Speak to my brothers
so that they will divide the goods
of my Father with me.
Jesus answered him:
Who has made of me a man of division?
And turning to his disciples,
he said to them:
Who am I to divide?

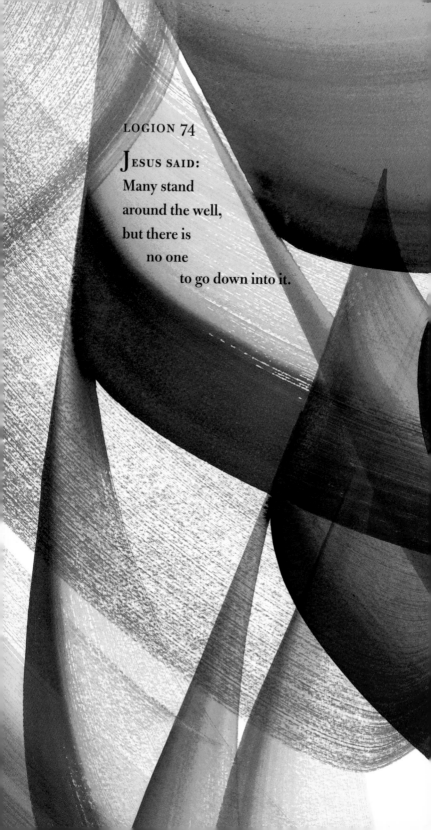

LOGION 74

JESUS SAID:
Many stand
around the well,
but there is
no one
to go down into it.

MONAXOC

LOGION 75

J ESUS SAID:
Many stand before the door
but it is the solitary ones
and those who have become simple
who will enter the bridal chamber.

ΠЄϪЄΙ̅Ϲ̅ϪЄΛΝΟΚΠ
ЄΠΟΥΟЄΙΠΛЄΙЄΤ
ϹΙϪШΟΥΤΗΡΟΥΛΝ
ΟΚΠЄΠΤΗΡΥΝ̅ΤΛΠ
ΤΗΡΥЄΙЄΒΟΛΝ̅Ϲ̅ΗΤ
ΛΥШΝ̅ΤΛΠΤΗΡΥΠШ

LOGION 77

Jᴇsᴜs sᴀɪᴅ:
I am the Light
which illumines all men.
I am the All.
The All came forth from me
and the All ended up in me.
Split some wood, I am there.
Lift a stone,
you will find me there.

LOGION 94

JESUS SAID:
He who seeks
will find.
To him who knocks
from the inside,
it will be opened.

LOGION 108

JESUS SAID:
He who drinks from my mouth will become
like me, and I shall be him,
and the hidden things will be revealed to him.

πεχειτ

LOGION 113

THE DISCIPLES SAID to Jesus:
The Kingdom,
when will it come?
Jesus answered:
It is not by watching for it
that you will see it come.
No one will say: behold, it is there
or it is here.
The Kingdom of the Father
is spread over all the earth
and men do not see it.

FRANK LALOU

WHEN MY BOOK *La Calligraphie de l'Invisible* (*The Calligraphy of the Invisible*) came out in 1994, many of my Jewish friends considered it an anomaly that a book whose main focus was Hebraic calligraphy should begin with a chapter called "The Gospel of Thomas: Writing One's Life." Nonetheless, from the time I was seventeen years old, when my philosophy professor placed this work in my hands, I knew with an intimate knowledge that it would become my *livre de chevet*, my bedside book. I give this term a biblical connotation. *Chevet* means "head," and the first word in the Bible is literally "at the head," *bereshit*, "in the beginning." It was to become the book of my beginnings.

Each day I drew from it a source of meditation, of wisdom, and of stupefaction. Many of the logia seemed incomprehensible to me. But the more obscure they were, the more I loved them. The void they created in me following each reading plunged me into an intoxicating state of perplexity.

The Gospel of Thomas was able to touch my Hebraic sensibility because it was without reference to the life of Jesus, without allusion to the Virgin Mary, without apology for suffering. Here Jesus was a great spiritual master. In the one hundred and fourteen teachings of this Pharisaic Jewish rabbi, I felt the presence of the entire teaching of the Talmud and of another Jewish master, Hillel—that representative of the gentle and open aspect of Jewish thought. Logion 42 ("Jesus said: be passers-by") sent me back to my own Jewishness. Moreover, if you go back to the Hebrew or the Aramaic spoken by Jesus, this logion would be translated like this: "Be Hebrew," because "Hebrew" means "he who passes." In this aphorism, Jesus invites the Jews, the Judaeans, to become Hebrews. To be Hebrew means to accept the full fragility of the human condition; it means to create solidity on the basis of that fragility. It means to be attentive to all the signs placed on the passer-by's route, to be attentive to the other. To be Hebrew is not to have a place to lay one's head. Here the lot of Jesus and that of the Hebrews converged.

In 1986, with my career as a calligrapher hardly under way, I decided to take a leap forward by creating a major work. I was still a teacher at the time. Taking advantage of the summer vacation, I left for Greece. There, under the pines, in the shade of the olive trees, in the little recesses of hotel rooms, I calligraphed the Gospel of Thomas. One hundred and fourteen maxims, one hundred and fourteen calligraphic plates, an immense labor. At the end of this, I was so completely enthralled by the sayings of this Yeshuah (Jesus) and of this play of letters that I forgot everything else. When the summer was over, I returned to France with my gospel under my arm. I asked an art critic who had encouraged my early work to provide me with some connections for promoting and selling my book. I placed the work in a ceramic box that contained a sculpture by Dominique Cour. It took two people to lift it.

Then my life began to change. In the same week, I received a letter informing me that the board of education had granted me a year's sabbatical with salary; and on top of this, a woman telephoned me asking to see the Gospel of Thomas that I had just completed. The following day at her home, I slowly showed her my book. She was thoroughly seduced by the work. She was not shocked by its price, enormous for me in those days, and she bought it from me immediately. Afterward, she asked me to interpret a series of dreams she had had over the previous three nights in which she had seen a perfectly delineated symbol. She took a piece of paper and drew it. At once I was plunged into a state of stupefaction, because what she had just drawn was the geometrical figure that the sculptor Cour engraved on all his works.

She had had absolutely no opportunity to catch a glimpse of this figure during the times I was opening and closing the ceramic box. In this way the element of the fantastic brutally forced its way into my life.

And now creating twenty-four new calligraphies to illustrate logia of the Gospel of Thomas gave me an opportunity to reconnect with this experience of my youth. Once again I traveled to Greece, to a lost corner of the Peloponnesus where you look out upon the olive trees and the islands of the southern Adriatic. I had with me my pens, my inks, my paper, my manuals of Coptic—everything I needed to plunge again into the ceaselessly self-renewing ocean of the sayings of the Jewish master.

Conceived of as calligraphic reference points, the letter *tau*, the Eastern writing styles, the Coptic alphabet, and labyrinths are what have guided my creations all through the present volume.

For more than two years now, in all nearly all my calligraphies, the letter *tau* has supplied the basic rhythm of my plates. The beginning of my idyll with this character surely lay with the French word *toi*, of which I gave a rendering in several of my books. All by itself, the letter *T* epitomizes all the calligraphic gestures, because it contains within it the two essential forms of this art: the curve and the straight line, the belly and the upright. Expressing the encounter of horizontality and verticality, for me the *tau* is a quest for the other, human or invisible. The intersection of the curve and the straight line is clearly marked; the two fields of ink overlapping in this place in effect form a parallelepiped of the most saturated pigment. Richness is generated at the intersection of these two forces. To render them, I use oversize pens that I make myself, between five and twenty centimeters across at the nib, thus multiplying by a factor of several hundreds the normal size of a character. My obsessive work on the *T* also came about through my encounter with Lana paper, new for me at the time, because thanks to its texture, the crossing of the two lines was rendered in a more dramatic fashion. In Christianity, the *T* is the symbol of the cross of Jesus. I take only a remote interest in the symbolic significance of letters. A letter moves me not because of what it symbolizes but because of its form, its harmony, its proportions. My vision of letters is more erotic than metaphysical.

The collection of calligraphies in this book has two themes: Western developments with the *tau* as the main figure and Eastern developments of abstract gestures executed with my Nara brushes that I brought back from my journey to Japan. What is the reason for the presence of the Japanese gestural style in this volume? The first time that I calligraphed the Gospel of Thomas, I was already practicing Zen. It seemed to me that a number of the logia in the Gospel had the quality of veritable koans, paradoxical phrases that plunge us into abysses of interpretive thought. To grasp their meaning is to gain access to another type of perception of reality—the disciple is forced to give up his habitual tool of rationality and discursiveness.

Since I spoke Greek and had practiced a method of Greek calligraphy, it was not difficult for me to approach Coptic, which uses an alphabet composed of the twenty-four Hellenic letters and seven others drawn from demotic Egyptian. The word *copt* is an Arabic term, itself derived from the Greek *Aigyptos*, which was used to designate the inhabitants of Egypt. Derived from hieroglyphics, hieratic and demotic Egyptian correspond to the final stages of development of the ancient Egyptian script. As the usual script of the scribes, the hieratic script was used in the composition of administrative documents but also for scientific, literary, and religious texts. Starting with the seventh century BCE, it was no longer used for the transcription of the sacred texts, and the demotic script replaced it for documents related to everyday life. It was not until some time in the third century that the Egyptians borrowed the twenty-four characters of the Greek alphabet and added to them seven letters of the demotic script to constitute their own alphabet for their language, Coptic.

However, the alphabet used for the Gospel of Thomas only includes six letters in addition to the Greek ones. The form of the Greek letters is

ⲱ ⲩ ⳉ ⳋ ⳋ ⲧ

shaï   fâi   hori   janja   guima   ti

The six supplementary letters of the
Coptic script in The Gospel of Thomas.

very close to that of
the uncials used in the
books of the fourth and
fifth centuries.

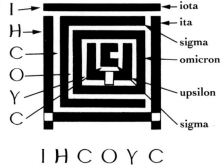

From the very begin-
ning, my work has been
filled with labyrinths.
I've made jewelry out
of them as well as marquetery and designs for gardens.
Embedding characters within each other has always
been one of my passions. Throughout time, the Chi-
nese, the Arabs, the Jews, but also the Latin calligra-
phers, have been attracted to this form, which is found
very little in contemporary calligraphy. The labyrinth

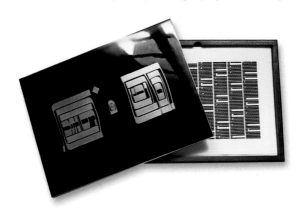

makes it possible to make a word unreadable, which gives it a secret, hidden value. The viewer thinks they are seeing an abstract form, even though a meaning is hidden in the lines. In the present book, I have "labyrinthized" the names of Jesus and Thomas to better express the esoteric and apocryphal character of this gospel.

Frank Lalou